Marjoram · Parsley · Nutmeg

Chives · Basil · C... · Ba

English Lavender · Black

d · Savory · Sage · Mint

permint · Saffron · Chile

· Sweet Violet · Commo

· Rose · Lemon Balm · R

arsley · Nutmeg · Cloves

il · Cilantro · Bay Leaf

Lavender · Black Pepper

Savory · Sage · Mint · Ta

int · Saffron · Chile Pepp

A Feast
of
Friendship

*A collection of recipes
to enjoy with friends*

A Special Gift

FOR:

....

FROM:

....

DATE:

Recipes

A Feast
of
Friendship

Recipes by Mark B. Willmert

Edited by Paul C. Brownlow

Brownlow

Brownlow Publishing Company, Inc.

Introduction

The joy of cooking means many things to
many different people, but one thing remains constant:
it is wonderful to share that joy with family and friends.

Have you ever been at a friend's house for a
special luncheon or dinner and tasted something
so good you just had to have the recipe?
If so, you'll love this cookbook and these creative recipes.
After all, that is where most of our
favorite recipes come from—our friends.

When you prepare these easy-to-make recipes,
you create good food with the extra flair and
seasoning that will draw rave reviews...and that
highest-of-all compliments, "I must have that recipe!"

Kitchen Prayer

Bless the meals that I prepare.

May they be seasoned from above

with Thy blessing and Thy grace,

but most of all Thy love.

Roasted Red Pepper Vinaigrette

MAKES 1 CUP

1 large red bell pepper

¼ cup red wine vinegar

2 teaspoons sugar

½ cup olive oil

1 clove fresh garlic

Salt & freshly ground pepper, to taste

TO ROAST PEPPER

- To roast pepper: preheat the broiler & line a baking sheet with aluminum foil. Place pepper 4 to 5 inches from the heat source & broil until the skin is charred black, 12 to 16 minutes. Remove pepper & place in pepper bag, close tightly, & let pepper steam for 10 to 15 minutes. Remove & slip off charred skins.
- Combine the roasted red pepper, vinegar, sugar, garlic, salt & pepper in a food processor; pulse on & off until the pepper is smoothly puréed. (If food processor is not available, mince garlic & red pepper as finely as possible.)
- With machine running, slowly drizzle in the oil & process until the oil is incorporated & the vinaigrette has slightly thickened. Cover & store in the refrigerator for up to 2 days. Bring to room temperature & stir vigorously before using.

This wonderfully sweet but tart vinaigrette will delight your guests—a perfect dressing for lettuce or pasta salads of any type. For a delicious appetizer, drizzle atop roasted pepper covered sourdough bread & broil.

Fresh Fruit with English Cream & Mint

SERVES 8

1½ vanilla beans

1 quart milk

8 egg yolks

1 cup sugar

Assorted seasonal fruit, sliced

Fresh mint leaves, julienne

A nice, light, colorful treat for any time of the day. Select your fruit according to what is in season or what best complements the occasion.

- Split vanilla beans in half & remove seeds. Place milk & beans in a small pan & boil over medium heat. Remove from heat.
- In a mixing bowl, blend egg yolks until color is light. Add ⅓ of the boiled milk to the egg mixture. Mix thoroughly.
- Add the egg mixture to the remaining ⅔ of the milk & return to heat, boiling for about 1 minute. Strain & cool.
- Place mixed fruit in a serving bowl & drizzle with sauce. Sprinkle with mint & serve. May garnish with whole mint sprigs around edge.

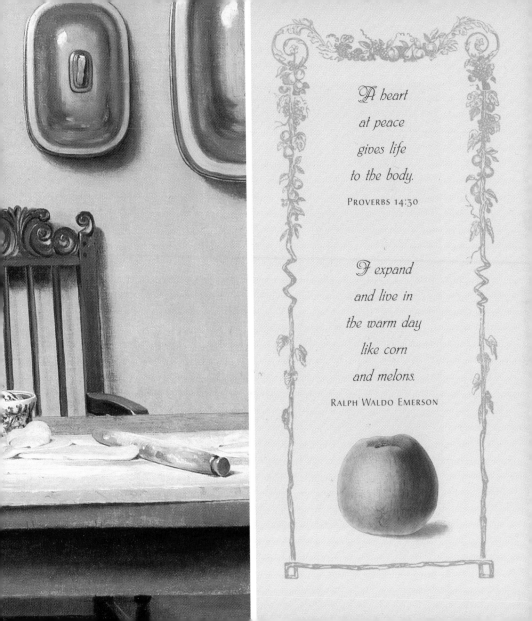

*A heart
at peace
gives life
to the body.*

PROVERBS 14:30

*I expand
and live in
the warm day
like corn
and melons.*

RALPH WALDO EMERSON

Homemade Hot Chocolate

SERVES 2

3 ounces bittersweet chocolate

2 cups milk

1 teaspoon all-purpose flour

- The chocolate is an important component in this recipe. The better the quality of the chocolate used, the better the taste.
- Finely chop the chocolate & place in a small saucepan with the milk. Placed over medium-high heat, & stir continuously with a wooden spoon until chocolate melts & the mixture comes to a boil. Remove the pan from the heat.
- Place the flour in a small bowl, briskly whisk ½ cup of the hot chocolate into the flour in a slow stream, & continue to whisk until the mixture is smooth. Whisk this mixture back into the hot chocolate & once again bring to a boil, whisking constantly.
- Serve hot & enjoy. Shave some remaining chocolate & sprinkle atop for an added touch.

Adults & children will come running on those cold winter days for your soon-to-be famous Homemade Hot Chocolate. A perfect treat any time of the day, keep ingredients on hand for those impromptu visits.

Lemon Buttermilk Corn Muffins

MAKES 10 MUFFINS

1 egg

1 tablespoon lemon juice

1 tablespoon grated lemon zest

5 tablespoons melted butter

2 tablespoons canola oil (corn oil if desired)

1 cup buttermilk

1 cup all-purpose flour

1 cup yellow cornmeal

1½ teaspoons baking powder

½ teaspoon baking soda

¼ cup sugar

½ teaspoon salt

- Preheat oven to 400°. Grease cups of muffin tin with soft butter or a vegetable spray.

- Whisk together egg, lemon zest, lemon juice, melted butter & oil in a large bowl. Whisk in buttermilk. Mix the flour, cornmeal, baking powder, baking soda, sugar & salt in a separate bowl. Add the flour mixture to the buttermilk mixture & stir gently with a rubber spatula until just blended.

- Pour batter into muffin tin, filling ¾ full. Bake for approximately 15 minutes or until done (until edges begin to pull away from side of the cup). Remove from tin & serve.

A sure winner any time of the day. Serve warm with your favorite preserve or honey.

Let the heavens rejoice, let the earth be glad;

let the fields be jubilant, and everything in them.

PSALM 96:11,12

Before green apples blush,

Before green nuts embrown,

Why, one day in the country

Is worth a month in town.

CHRISTINA ROSSETTI

They serve God well who serve His creatures.

CAROLINE NORTON

Spice a dish with love and it pleases every palate.

PLAUTUS

Baked Cinnamon Apples

SERVES 4

½ cup sugar

1 teaspoon ground cinnamon

½ teaspoon freshly ground nutmeg

2 cups apple cider

¼ teaspoon vanilla extract

½ teaspoon minced lemon zest

4 apples, washed & dried

· Preheat oven to 300°. Mix together the sugar, cinnamon & nutmeg. Combine the cider, vanilla & lemon zest. Core apples without cutting through the bottom. Leaving a 1 inch wide band, peel top of the apple. Place apples in a baking dish & fill apples with the sugar mixture. Pour cider mixture into baking dish & cover.

· Bake apples for 30 minutes, basting with cider several times. Using a paring knife, pierce largest apple to see if it is tender. Continue baking until done (will vary based on size & type of apple). Serve warm.

The aroma of this dessert baking will lure all into your kitchen with a nose of curiosity. Marvelous when served with ice cream.

Grandma's Tomato Bisque

SERVES 4

½ cup onions

½ cup unsalted butter

1 tablespoon dill weed

1 teaspoon dill seed

2 teaspoons oregano

5 cups canned crushed whole tomatoes

4 cups chicken stock

2 tablespoons flour

⅓ cup parsley, chopped

2 tablespoons honey

1¼ cups heavy cream

⅔ cup half & half sour cream

Salt & white pepper to taste

- In a large pot, sauté onions in 6 tablespoons butter along with dill seed, dill weed & oregano for 4 to 5 minutes or until onions become translucent. Add chicken stock & crushed tomatoes.

- Blend 2 tablespoons butter & 2 tablespoons flour, constantly whisking over medium heat for 3 minutes without browning.

- Add roux to stock & whisk to blend. Add salt & pepper. Bring to a boil, stirring occasionally to avoid burning.

- Reduce heat and simmer for 18 minutes. Add remaining ingredients. Remove from heat & purée. Strain. Serve as desired.

This variation of the classic tomato soup is a staple in many homes. Whether topped with sour cream or garnished with fresh parsley, this recipe is enjoyable year round.

Good character, like good soup, is made at home.

Your greatest pleasure is that which

rebounds from hearts that you have made glad.

HENRY WARD BEECHER

Fresh Grapefruit Spritz

MAKES 4 DRINKS

2 cups fresh grapefruit juice (2 pink grapefruit)

1 tablespoon sugar

Ice cubes

1 large bottle (24 ounces) sparkling water

4 fresh pineapple spears, for garnish

4 fresh mint sprigs, for garnish

Optional: 2 tablespoons grenadine

- Combine grapefruit juice, water, grenadine & sugar in a large pitcher. Mix thoroughly.
- Fill glasses with ice & pour mixture into glass. Garnish each drink with a pineapple spear & a sprig of mint. Serve & enjoy!
- Try blending this drink with ice for a summer frozen treat. Feel free to add other fruit juices for a different flavor.

Along with those long, warm summer afternoons comes the time of enjoying a refreshing drink with friends. Whether on the gazebo, patio or under the shade of a tree, this cool drink is sure to refresh everyone's spirits.

Good apple pies are a considerable part

of our domestic happiness.

JANE AUSTEN

In an orchard there should be enough to eat,

enough to lay up, enough to be stolen,

and enough to rot upon the ground.

JAMES BOSWELL

Build houses and settle down;

plant gardens and eat what they produce.

JEREMIAH 29:5

Grilled Zesty Prawns

MAKES 6

2 fresh garlic cloves, minced

1 roasted serrano chile pepper, peeled & seeded

1 bunch cilantro, chopped

3 fresh lemons, juiced

1 bunch of green onions, diced

1 anaheim or ancho chile

2 cups peanut or olive oil

24 jumbo prawns, peeled

Serving this could easily become a favorite tradition. Whether for a meal or an appetizer, this quick recipe will spice up any type of get-together or special occasion.

- Depending on how you buy your shrimp, you may have to remove the outer shell & rinse. Try leaving the tail on for a nice presentation.
- Combine the garlic, serrano pepper, cilantro, lemon juice & scallions in a large mixing bowl.
- Cut or tear the ancho chile into the marinade mixture & toss. Add ½ the oil & pour over prawns. Add remaining oil as necessary to coat the prawns evenly, while avoiding floating them in marinade. Marinate for 2 hours.
- Grill for 1½ minutes on each side & serve. For grilling ease, feel free to place these shrimp on small skewers. Beware: shrimp cook quickly.

A lunch of bread and cheese after a good walk is more enjoyable than a Lord Mayor's feast.

SIR JOHN LUBBOCK

Give us this day our daily bread.

MATTHEW 6:11

Children are the hands by which we take hold of heaven.

HENRY WARD BEECHER

Taste and see that the Lord is good.

PSALM 34:8

English Trifle

MAKES 8 SERVINGS

3 egg yolks

3 tablespoons sugar

1 cup milk

3-ounce package unfilled ladyfingers

6 tablespoons *Lady Caroline Raspberry Preserve*

12 amaretti cookies, coarsely crushed (1 cup)

2 tablespoons toasted almonds, slivered

1/3 cup orange juice

1 cup whipping cream

2 tablespoons confectioners' sugar

Undoubtedly the most popular of English desserts. Use a glass or crystal bowl to display the beauty of this delicious delight.

- Using a small bowl, whisk egg yolks & sugar until thickened & pale. In a small heavy saucepan, heat milk over low heat until tiny bubbles appear around the edges. Gradually whisk milk into the yolk mixture. Pour custard into a clean, small heavy saucepan. Cook & stir over low heat for 3 to 4 minutes or until custard is slightly thickened & coats the back of a metal spoon. Immediately place in a container of ice water to cool. Occasionally stir to prevent a skin from forming.

- To assemble, spread flat sides of 1 strip of ladyfingers with 3 tablespoons of the preserve. Top with the remaining strip, flat side down. Cut the ladyfingers apart & arrange to cover the bottom & sides of glass bowl. You may cut in ½ if necessary. Sprinkle with the amaretti cookie crumbs, then almonds. Drizzle with orange juice, then spoon in the cooled custard. Whip the cream & spread it over all. Cover & refrigerate overnight.
- To serve, in a small bowl stir remaining preserve until smooth & runny. Drop spoonfuls onto the whipped cream & with a pointed knife tip "pull" them through the cream to obtain a marble effect. Enjoy!

Butternut Soup

SERVES 6

2 tablespoons butter

1 medium yellow onion, peeled & chopped

2 stalks celery, chopped

3 medium carrots, peeled & chopped

1 medium butternut squash, peeled & seeded

3 large bay leaves

2 teaspoons thyme

½ teaspoon anise seed

1 teaspoon marjoram

4 cups chicken stock

½ cup heavy cream

Salt & white pepper to taste

Warm up family & friends with this rich, aromatic soup. The beautiful color & texture are perfect for garnishing with gently heated cranberries or even a sprig of fresh herbs.

- Using a 3 quart saucepan, melt butter. Add the onion, celery & carrots. Cook slowly without browning until items are softened. Cut the butternut squash into chunks & add to saucepan followed by the herbs, chicken stock, & a dash of salt & pepper. Cover & bring to a boil. Reduce heat & simmer until squash becomes tender.
- Purée the soup in a food processor & return to clean saucepan. Bring to a boil. Remove from heat & stir in the cream. Salt & pepper to taste. Serve.

The soul that
perpetually overflows
with kindness
and compassion
will always
be cheerful.

PARKE GODWIN

A kitchen is a
friendly place,
Full of living's
daily grace.

To a friend's house
the way is never long.

Baked Brie with Edible Flowers

ALLOW 3 OUNCES BRIE PER PERSON

1 large wheel of Brie

¼ cup mint or apple jelly

Fresh thyme

Fresh chives

Edible fresh flowers

- In a small saucepan, gently melt mint or apple jelly. Brush on top of Brie wheel that has been brought to room temperature.
- Place wheel in oven at 200° for 5 minutes.
- Remove from oven & arrange edible flowers (available at most grocery stores), chives & herbs as desired. Serve with baguettes or crackers.

Simple to make, beautiful to serve. Let your creative desires take over in designing the floral arrangement adorning your wheel of creamy Brie. Your guests will be as amazed by its beauty as by its delectable taste. Serve with baguettes, crackers of all types, or any other treat your heart desires.

Recipe for Happiness

Combine 4 parts of Contentment, 2 parts of Joy,
and 1 part Pleasure. But these ingredients
must be grown in one's own garden.
Sometimes they may be obtained of a Good Friend.
When so procured, a fair return must be made
else Happiness spoils and becomes trouble.

Sometimes Discontent and Ambition have been
combined in a desire to obtain Happiness,
but Fame and Wealth have resulted,
and persons who have tasted these
say they are inferior substitutes.

Baked Artichoke & Sun-dried Tomato Spread

SERVES 6

½ cup mayonnaise

4 cups Parmesan cheese, grated

1 can artichoke hearts, sectioned

1 large garlic clove, minced

3 sun-dried tomatoes, chopped

Dash of salt

- Prepare ingredients & mix thoroughly together in a small bowl. Place mixture into your desired oven-proof service.
- Preheat oven to 350° & bake for 25 to 30 minutes. Serve with any type of bread or cracker. Wonderful when made in a cutout sourdough round.

One bite is never enough for this popular appetizer! People will keep coming back for more. This dish is easy to make & very versatile as to what it can be served on or with.

The best and most beautiful
things in the world
cannot be seen or even touched.
They must be felt with the heart.

HELEN KELLER

No one is useless in this world
who lightens the burden of it for anyone else.

CHARLES DICKENS

What brings joy to the heart is not so much
the friend's gift as the friend's love.

ST. AELRED OF RIEVAULX

The only security for happiness is
to have a mind filled with the love
of the infinite and the eternal.

SPINOZA

You don't have a garden just for yourself.
You have it to share.

AUGUSTA CARTER

Where there is no extravagance
there is no love,
and where there is no love
there is no understanding.

OSCAR WILDE

Creamy Chicken & Mushrooms

SERVES 6

6 boneless, skinless chicken breasts

2 tablespoons butter or margarine

10 ounces fresh mushrooms, sliced

1 bunch green onions, sliced

1/3 cup light mayonnaise

2/3 cup light sour cream

1 cup dijon mustard

1/2 cup toasted, chopped walnuts

This dish is easy to make & can be served in a variety of fashions. Try it over a bed of rice, pasta, or even your favorite vegetables.

- In skillet, sauté chicken in butter 8 to 10 minutes or until done, turning occasionally. Remove & keep warm.
- Add mushrooms & onions to skillet, sauté 3 to 4 minutes or until golden. Stir in mayonnaise, sour cream & dijon mustard. Continuously stirring, cook over low heat 6 to 9 minutes or until heated through. Stir in walnuts. Spoon over chicken.
- A wonderful dish to serve over a bed of rice or pasta.

Parmesan Eggplant Dumplings

SERVES 4

1 large eggplant

1 cup olive oil

2 eggs

⅓ cup Parmesan cheese, grated

1⅓ cups flour

Dash of oregano

Dash of thyme

Salt & freshly ground pepper, to taste

A great appetizer to get that memorable evening off to the right start. Can be served with a variety of dipping sauces to assure that everyone has a choice they enjoy.

- Peel eggplant, then cut into cubes. Sauté eggplant in olive oil for approximately 15 minutes over low heat, but do not let the eggplant turn brown. Drain eggplant on paper towels & allow to cool.
- In a mixing bowl, combine the eggs, Parmesan, flour, oregano & thyme. Season with salt & pepper. Add the cooled eggplant & place the mixture into a pastry bag.
- In a large pot, add water & a little olive oil, & bring to a boil. Squeeze the eggplant mixture out of the pastry bag & cut into 1 inch pieces. Drop into boiling water for about 2 minutes each. The dumplings will rise to the top of the water when they are cooked.
- Serve on a platter with your favorite dipping sauce.

You say that this world to you seems drained of its sweets! I don't know what you call sweet. Honey and the honeycomb, roses and violets, are yet in the earth. The sun and moon yet reign in heaven, and the stars keep up their pretty twinklings. Meats and drinks, sweet sights and sweet smells, a country walk, spring and autumn, follies and repentance, quarrels and reconcilements have all a sweetness by turns. Good humor and good nature, friends at home that love you, and friends abroad that miss you—you possess all these things, and more innumerable, and these are all sweet things. You may extract honey from everything.

CHARLES LAMB

Grilled Balsamic Baby Carrots

SERVES 6

2 bunches baby carrots, peeled

⅓ cup balsamic vinegar

Fresh thyme

Dash of salt

- Wash & peel carrots, leaving the greens on the top attached. Using a small knife, cut 4 parallel lines into each side of carrot without cutting all the way through (this will allow vinegar flavor to soak in).
- Place carrots in shallow container & pour balsamic vinegar, fresh thyme & salt on top. Allow to marinate for at least 2 hours.
- Place carrots on the edge of the grill & cook until tender. You may remove carrot tops if desired, but they make a great garnish when left on.

Whether served as an appetizer or a side vegetable for your main dish, this basic recipe will take little effort but gain much praise. With the greens left on top, each plate will be beautifully garnished & friends will have found a new favorite recipe.

Spiced Raisin Bread

MAKES 1 LOAF

2 cups flour

2 teaspoons baking powder

1 teaspoon salt

1 teaspoon cinnamon

½ teaspoon ground nutmeg

⅔ cup brown sugar, firmly packed

1 cup raisins

¾ cup old-fashioned oats

¼ cup shortening

2 eggs, beaten

1 cup milk

- Combine flour, baking powder, salt, cinnamon
  & nutmeg. Add brown sugar, raisins, oats,
  shortening, eggs & milk & stir until just blended.
- Preheat oven to 350°. Pour batter into a
  greased loaf pan & bake for 55 to 60 minutes.
  Immediately remove from pan & cool on a
  wire rack.

This fragrant bread is loaded with spices & flavor for holidays or family Sunday afternoons. Eat warm or wrap & let cool for easier slicing. For that extra-special gathering, treat everyone by serving with cinnamon butter.

In the noise and clatter of my kitchen,
while people are at the same time
calling for different things,
I possess God in as great tranquility
as if I were upon my knees.

BROTHER LAWRENCE

Love does not dominate; it cultivates.

JOHANN WOLFGANG VON GOETHE

The heart of the giver
makes the gift dear and precious.

MARTIN LUTHER

Banana Cinnamon Pancakes

SERVES 4

1 cup all-purpose flour

1¼ teaspoons baking powder

½ teaspoon ground cinnamon

Pinch of salt

¼ cup brown sugar, packed

3 tablespoons corn oil

1 large egg

1 teaspoon pure vanilla extract

1 cup ripe bananas, mashed (2 to 3 bananas)

1 tablespoon butter, melted

Whether for breakfast or for dessert, these banana pancakes are sure to warm both heart & palate of your family & friends. Wonderful served with cinnamon butter & maple syrup.

- Combine flour, baking powder, cinnamon, salt & brown sugar in a large mixing bowl.
- In a different bowl mix together the milk, sugar, 2 tablespoons of the oil, egg & vanilla extract. Add to the dry ingredients & stir until the mixture is almost smooth. Fold the bananas into the batter. Loosely cover & let rest for 20 minutes.
- Combine melted butter & oil in small bowl to use while cooking pancakes.
- Place a skillet (preferably nonstick) over medium heat. Place a small portion of butter & oil mixture in skillet & heat. Pour ¼ cup batter per pancake into skillet & cook until small bubbles form on the top, about 1 minute. Flip the pancake over & cook an additional 45 seconds. Repeat procedure with remainder of batter. Serve warm with your desired topping.

*Friends cherish
each other's hopes.
They are kind
to each other's dreams.*

HENRY DAVID THOREAU

*Serve one another
in love.*

GALATIANS 5:13

*Friendship
is in loving
rather than in
being loved.*

ROBERT BRIDGES

Dill Lemon Cauliflower

Serves 6

1 head cauliflower

1 fresh lemon, juiced

⅓ cup unsalted butter

1 teaspoon dill seed

4 tablespoons dill weed

Dash of salt

- Separate cauliflower heads into florets & wash. Set aside & allow to dry.
- Melt butter & combined with lemon juice, dill seed, dill weed & salt. Place cauliflower in a casserole & pour liquid mixture on top.
- Preheat oven at 300° & place covered casserole in oven for approximately 30 minutes or until tender. (Cauliflower can be eaten raw, so the length of your cooking can vary to your desired taste.) Stir casserole & serve.
- You may use lemon wedges or fresh dill weed for a lovely garnish. This recipe may also be made on a stovetop.

When you're short on time but still want to do something special, this delightful vegetable side dish will add aroma to your kitchen while affording you extra time to get everything else prepared.

CAULIFLOWER
SNOWBALL

PUT UP BY
THE WAYNE SEED CO.
Fort Wayne, Ind.

Autumn Harvest Chicken Salad

SERVES 6

3 large Granny Smith apples, thinly sliced

1/3 cup blue cheese, crumbled

5 tablespoons chopped walnuts

1 large head romaine lettuce, washed, trimmed

1 bunch watercress, trimmed

2 cups smoked chicken, thinly sliced

Salt & freshly ground pepper, to taste

Freshly ground nutmeg, to taste

VINAIGRETTE

1 tablespoon dijon mustard

1/4 cup white wine vinegar

1/2 cup extra-virgin olive oil

1 teaspoon dill

1/4 teaspoon cinnamon

1/2 teaspoon freshly ground nutmeg

1 teaspoon sugar

Salt & freshly ground pepper, to taste

Nutmeg adds a highly aromatic, sweetish taste to this colorful salad. Smoked chicken may be substituted because the flavor of a smoked meat blends beautifully with the deep spices flavor. Try different types of lettuce or apple for pleasing variations.

- Vinaigrette: combine mustard, vinegar, dill cinnamon, nutmeg, sugar, salt & pepper. While whisking constantly, very slowly add oil. Stir vigorously before using.
- In a bowl, combine apple slices, blue cheese, walnuts & 4 tablespoons vinaigrette. Mix, cover & refrigerate for up to 8 hours.
- To serve, arrange lettuce, watercress & chilled apple mixture on a platter. Add chicken & drizzle vinaigrette on top. Season with salt, fresh pepper & fresh nutmeg.

Baked Mushroom Caps

SERVES 6

1 package large mushrooms, small if desired

4 ounces cream cheese

2 medium garlic cloves, minced

6 chives, minced

1 teaspoon fresh thyme

¼ teaspoon paprika

- After cleaning mushrooms, separate mushroom stems from caps & set caps aside. Mince 2 or 3 of the mushroom stems & use remaining stems as you desire.
- After cream cheese has reached room temperature, put all ingredients, including minced stems, into a small mixing bowl. Mix throughly until you have a soft, creamy consistency.
- Preheat oven to 350°. Using a spoon, add mixture to hollow of mushroom cap where stem was removed. Place on a baking sheet covered with aluminum foil & bake for 12 to 14 minutes. Sprinkle with paprika, serve warm.

Your guests will enjoy these tasty delights, & you will find yourself creating this easy-to-make recipe time and time again. For that special touch, sprinkle the edge of your serving platter with paprika.

emary · Thyme · Dill · M
Garlic · White Pepper · C
min · Coriander · Fennel
k · Oregano · Mustard Se
Spearmint · Paprika · Pe
emon Grass · Anise · Tu
erican Elderberry · Sorre
yme · Dill · Marjoram
White Pepper · Chives · B
oriander · Fennel · Englis
Oregano · Mustard Seed
armint · Paprika · Pepper